ECO
STEAM

the
# FOOD
# WE EAT

## GEORGIA AMSON-BRADSHAW

WAYLAND
www.waylandbooks.co.uk

First published in Great Britain in 2018 by Wayland

Copyright © Hodder and Stoughton Limited, 2018

 Produced for Wayland by
White-Thomson Publishing Ltd
www.wtpub.co.uk

Series Editor: Georgia Amson-Bradshaw
Series Designer: Rocket Design (East Anglia) Ltd

ISBN: 978 1 5263 0731 6
10 9 8 7 6 5 4 3 2 1

Wayland
An imprint of
Hachette Children's Group
Part of Hodder & Stoughton
Carmelite House
50 Victoria Embankment
London EC4Y 0DZ

An Hachette UK Company
www.hachette.co.uk
www.hachettechildrens.co.uk

Printed in China

Picture acknowledgements:
B Brown 4b, curiosity 5t, volkansengor 5b, khryzov 7t, FatCamera 7b, TheWorst 8t, emholk 9t, megastocker 9b, Oleksandra Naumenko 10t, Tomacco 10l, lukeruk 15b, jennyt 16t, VartB 16b, Vladislav Gajic 17t, Amantes_amentis 17c, amathers 17b, Natali Snailcat 18b, Voropaev Vasiliy 19b, Illustratiostock 20t, stnazkul 21t, Lano Lan 24t, feiyuezhangjie 24b, gemredding 25c, gala_gala 26l, wanpatsorn 26r, Richard Whitcombe 27t, petovarga 27c, Aedka Studio 27b, Rawpixel 28bl, marugod83 28tr, FangXiaNuo 28tl, wavebreakmedia 28br, photokup 31b, Lisa S. 32t, Tim M 32b, Andrei Verner 33t, DN1988 33b, Danyliuk Konstantine 34t, nelya43 34b, LiliiaKyrylenko 35t, PRO Stock Professional 35b, Looker_Studio 40l, stockcreations 41b, Alex_Traksel 41c, kRie 46t, Everett Historical 46c, Qvasimodo art 46b

Illustrations on pages 23 and 39 by Steve Evans.

All design elements from Shutterstock.

Every effort has been made to clear copyright. Should there be any inadvertent omission, please apply to the publisher for rectification.

The website addresses (URLs) included in this book were valid at the time of going to press. However, it is possible that contents or addresses may have changed since the publication of this book. No responsibility for any such changes can be accepted by either the author and or the publisher.

!

Always ask
an adult for
permission before
using any kitchen
equipment including
knives or the hob.

# CONTENTS

# FOOD, WASTE AND CLIMATE CHANGE

Food is one of our most basic necessities. But right now the way we produce our food around the world is not sustainable. This means that if we continue to do things the way we do now, in time we won't be able to feed everyone, due to damage to the climate and the Earth's ecosystems.

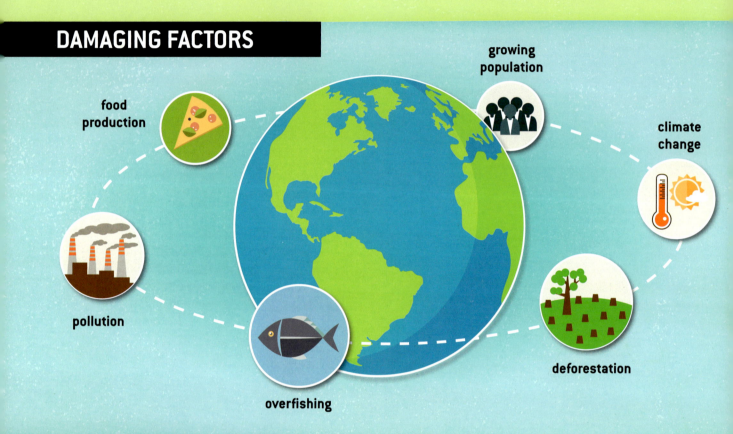

growing population

food production

climate change

pollution

overfishing

deforestation

## Changing our climate

One of the biggest issues caused by the way we currently produce food is the contribution our food industry makes to climate change. In particular, farming animals for food contributes a lot of greenhouse gases such as carbon dioxide, nitrous oxide and methane gas to the atmosphere. Gases are released in various ways, for instance as waste gases from the animals themselves, as a by-product of chemical fertilisers used to grow animal feed and as emissions from farm vehicles.

## Greenhouse effect

The increasing levels of greenhouse gases in the atmosphere are trapping heat from the Sun, and causing the Earth to heat up. This in turn is changing weather patterns around the world, creating severe droughts in some areas and dangerous and damaging storms in others.

## What a waste

Food waste and packaging waste are other big problems caused by the way we buy and use food. In the UK, about a third of the food that people buy is thrown away without being used, and much fresh produce comes packaged in plastic that also goes straight to landfill instead of being recycled. This landfill ends up releasing toxic chemicals into the surrounding soil or waterways, as well as creating more methane.

## Time for change

We need to change the way we produce, transport and package all sorts of foodstuffs in order to ensure we keep our planet in balance, and the Earth's living things – including humans and wildlife – healthy.

# THE BIG ISSUES

Although we currently produce enough food worldwide to feed everyone, it is not distributed equally. Unequal access to food means around 815 million people are going hungry, while 600 million others are suffering from obesity and health problems related to it. On top of this, the Earth's population is due to grow by two billion people by 2050, putting an even greater strain on our food production systems.

## UNEQUAL FOOD DISTRIBUTION

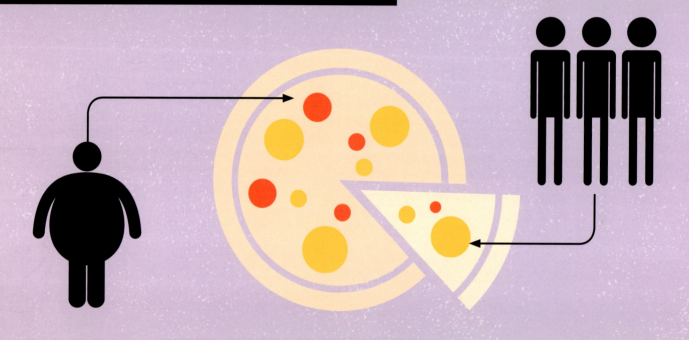

## Food choices

Even in countries that have adequate access to healthy food, our preferences can create challenges. In well-off countries, we have come to expect that all types of fresh food should be available all year round, and many of us prefer a diet that is high in meat and dairy products. Transporting fresh foods around the globe contributes to climate change, as do the animal-product-heavy diets that many people enjoy.

## A better future

The good news is we do have the power and the knowledge to solve these problems. All we need to do is work together to tackle them. Getting everyone to work together will require more people to understand the problems, as well as the sustainable alternatives, so the first step is spreading the word. It starts with people like you!

## Making a difference

In this book, find out about some specific issues and discover some STEAM solutions to those issues. Think about what changes you could make to your habits, or who you could tell about these ideas to make a difference, too.

Often the best solutions are found from looking at how nature deals with the same challenges.

# ANIMAL FARMING IMPACTS

Picture a hot meal in your head. What do you think of? A cheeseburger with chips and salad? A pizza covered in cheese and pepperoni? Roast chicken with vegetables and gravy? There is a good chance that any meal you imagine will contain a lot of meat, or dairy, or both. In well-off countries, we eat a lot of animal products, and our diets that are heavy in meat and dairy have a big impact on the Earth's climate and ecosystems.

## No room for wildlife

Agriculture is the largest type of human land use, covering almost half of Earth's land. But although a field full of animals or crops might not look like it harms the environment, appearances can be deceiving. Big monocrop fields (containing just one type of plant) don't provide homes or food for wildlife, and important habitats such as rainforests are being cleared every day to make more space for farming.

**Habitat loss is causing 150–200 new animal, plant and insect species to go extinct *every day*.**

**40%**

**SPOTLIGHT:** **ANIMAL PRODUCTS**

Meat, fish and dairy make up 40 per cent of what we eat in well-off countries.

## Inefficient system

Clearly humans need to eat, and we need a balanced diet that contains protein. But in terms of the Earth's resources, eating a lot of meat and dairy is a very inefficient way to meet our nutritional needs. Cattle eat up to 20 times more by weight in grain than they eventually produce in meat. This means that a meat-based meal uses far more land and other resources such as water to produce than a plant-based meal.

Currently, three quarters of agricultural land around the globe is used to raise animals or grow their food.

In order to feed the global population sustainably, people in well-off countries will need to reduce the amount of animal products in their diet.

## Climate change

Animal farming also generates a huge amount of methane, and other greenhouse gases including carbon dioxide and nitrous oxide. Although we are much more aware of the greenhouse gas emissions from cars and aeroplanes, animal farming contributes more greenhouse gases to the atmosphere than all of the world's transport combined.

# DIET AND NUTRITION

Our current diet is not good for the planet. But is it good for us? So what do we actually need to eat to stay healthy? A balanced diet is one that contains all the different nutrients our bodies need to power and repair themselves. There are six main parts of a balanced diet.

## Carbohydrates

These foods provide the most energy for the body's activities. Carbohydrates are found in many different foods, but typically are contained in foods such as bread, rice, pasta, grains and cereals, and in fruit and vegetables. Dietary fibre is also something you may have heard is important, as it helps keep everything moving through our digestive systems. It is found in many vegetables, beans and wholegrain wheat and oats.

**Fibre is a type of carbohydrate, but our bodies cannot break it down. It acts sort of like a broom, sweeping everything along with it through our guts!**

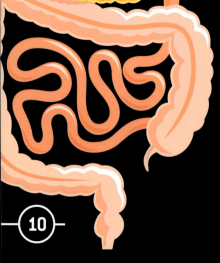

## Fats

We need small amounts of fat to give us energy, but also to help our body stay warm, and to help our body produce important hormones. Fats are found in nuts; some fruit such as avocados; and animal products.

# Protein

Another key element of our diet is protein. We use this to rebuild our bodies' cells, and make new muscle, bone, skin and organ tissue. Many people are aware that meat, eggs and dairy are good protein sources, but protein is also contained in plant foods including pulses (such as beans, lentils and peas) as well as nuts and seeds.

peas

nuts

lentils

# Vitamins

These are naturally-occurring chemicals that we need tiny amounts of, but are essential to stay healthy. Vitamins are mostly found in food, particularly fruit and vegetables, but some we get from other sources. For example, we make vitamin D ourselves when our skin is exposed to natural sunlight.

# Minerals

Like vitamins, we need very small amounts of minerals to do important jobs in our body, such as make new cells. Minerals are substances such as calcium or iron that come from rocks and metals, but we absorb them through our food, as plants (or the animals that have eaten the plants) contain them.

YOU ARE
80%
WATER!

# Water

We may not think of it as being part of our diet, but water is an essential thing we need to consume! Our bodies are 80 per cent water, so it's very important to stay hydrated.

**Many people take supplements to ensure they are getting all the minerals and vitamins they need.**

# SOLVE IT!

## DESIGN A BALANCED MENU

Using the animal-product-free dishes and ingredients shown on this page, can you come up with a tasty one-day meal plan including breakfast, lunch and dinner that contains all six essential elements of a balanced diet? You can add optional snacks, too, if you like.

### Pasta with tomato sauce

carbohydrate
vitamins and minerals

### PEANUT BUTTER ON TOAST

protein
carbohydrates
fat

### Cereal with enriched soy or nut milk

carbohydrate
vitamins and minerals

### Lentil and vegetable curry with rice

carbohydrate
protein
vitamins and minerals

### Roasted vegetables and hummus toastie

carbohydrate
vitamins and minerals
fat

### Fruit and nut flapjacks made with non-dairy spread

carbohydrate
protein
fat

## Mexican bean chilli wrap with guacamole

carbohydrate
protein
fat
vitamins and minerals

## FRUIT JUICE

water
vitamins and minerals

## Bean burgers with chips and salad

carbohydrate
protein
vitamins and minerals
fat

## Fruit salad

vitamins and minerals
carbohydrate

## Vegetable stir fry and noodles

carbohydrate
vitamins and minerals

# CAN YOU SOLVE IT?

BREAK FAST → LUNCH → DINNER

There are lots of different options to make a healthy meal plan covering breakfast, lunch and dinner on this page. Just check:

► You have included all the key elements of a balanced diet

► Your choice of dishes creates a varied meal plan for the day

For a delicious meal that could be part of your meal plan, see pages 14–15.

Take it further by researching other healthy dishes that don't use animal products, and eating plant-only foods for a day.

For menu ideas, go to page 42.

# TEST IT!
## MAKE BEAN BURGERS

These bean burgers are a good source of protein, and by making them yourself you can choose what flavours to include.
Always ask an adult before using sharp knives or the hob.

## YOU WILL NEED
(for 6 to 8 burgers)

one large or two medium sweet potatoes

240 g cooked black beans (drained)

100 g brown rice (about half a cup)

50 g ground almonds

about 5 spring onions, chopped

2 tsp smoked paprika

salt

1 tbsp vegetable oil

## TO SERVE:

burger buns
salad
sauce of your choice

## STEP ②

While the potatoes are in the oven, cook the brown rice according to the packet instructions.

## STEP ①

Cut the sweet potatoes in half and roast them cut-side down on a tray in a hot oven for 30 or 40 minutes until the insides are soft. When they are cooked, set them aside to cool.

## STEP ③

Put the drained black beans in the large bowl, and mash them up. Add the ground almonds, the chopped spring onion and the smoked paprika.

## STEP ④

When the rice is cooked, drain it if necessary and add it to the bowl.

## STEP ⑤

Scoop the soft insides out of the sweet potatoes and add to the bowl. Discard the skins.

## STEP ⑥

Mix everything in the bowl together. Add salt to taste.

## STEP ⑦

Shape spoonfuls of the mix into burger patties in your hands. You should get six to eight burgers from the mix.

## STEP ⑧

Heat the oil in a frying pan, and gently pan fry the burgers a couple at a time, until they are brown and crispy on the outside. This should take about five minutes per side.

**Serve the burgers in the buns with salad and a sauce of your choice.**

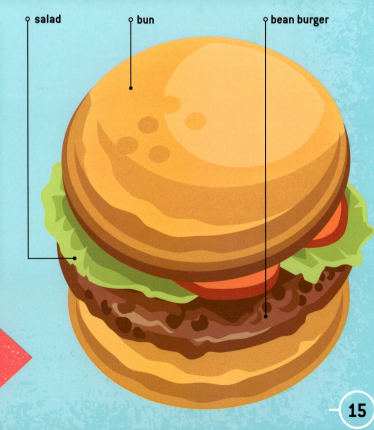

salad · bun · bean burger

# THE ISSUE:

# OVERFISHING

Most of our planet's surface is covered by the oceans, and they contain 80 per cent of all life on Earth. Around the world, millions of people depend on the oceans to provide them with food to eat and as the source of their livelihoods. Because the oceans are so big, it can seem like the resources they contain couldn't ever run out. Unfortunately, that is not the case.

## 90%

of the large predatory fish in the ocean that are eaten by humans, such as tuna and cod, have already disappeared.

## Wider effects

Overfishing is what happens when fish are removed from the sea, or from freshwater sources such as streams and rivers faster than they can naturally reproduce. Because certain species of fish are targeted, it disrupts natural food chains (see page 18). For example, without the fish to feed on, bigger animals such as seals and many sea birds are greatly decreasing in number.

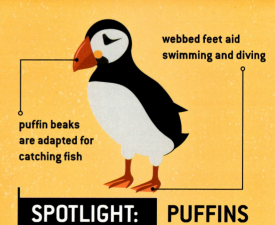

webbed feet aid swimming and diving

puffin beaks are adapted for catching fish

## SPOTLIGHT: PUFFINS

Puffins, which rely on ocean food chains, are at risk of extinction.

## Farmed fish

Around half the fish we eat worldwide comes from fish farms, where fish have been raised in tanks or large enclosures in lakes or in the ocean. However, fish farming does not automatically reduce the overfishing of wild fish.

**50%** FARMED

## Fish feed

The types of fish that are raised in farms are carnivorous species such as salmon. Huge amounts of smaller wild fish are taken from the oceans to feed the farmed fish. By taking so many of the small fish from further down the food chain, ecosystems in the oceans, lakes and rivers are increasingly disrupted.

**If we continue fishing at the same rate, *all* the world's fish stocks will collapse by 2048.**

## Water pollution

Farmed fish can also create a lot of water pollution. By keeping the fish in enclosed areas, a lot of waste is produced in the form of uneaten food and fish poo. This can be toxic for other plants and animals in the area.

# FOOD CHAINS AND ECOSYSTEMS

An ecosystem is made up of all the plants and animals that live in a particular place. The oceans contain many ecosystems, and the majority of species on Earth live in the oceans. Those marine plants and animals are all connected together in food chains and webs.

## An ocean chain

The chain starts with a producer (a plant) which is a living thing that can make food using energy from the Sun. Producers are eaten by consumers. In the ocean, microscopic plants called phytoplankton are eaten by zooplankton, which are tiny sea creatures. Zooplankton are then eaten by larger consumers, such as small fish. Small fish are eaten by bigger fish, such as mackerel. Bigger fish are eaten by animals including whales, seals and large sea birds.

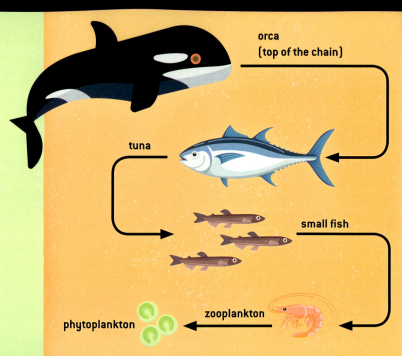

orca
(top of the chain)

tuna

small fish

phytoplankton

zooplankton

Coral reefs are very diverse ecosystems, containing complex food chains and webs.

# Connected webs

A food web is a way of showing that most creatures have more than one type of predator or prey, so they show up in several food chains. For example, an anchovy might be eaten by a gull, a mackerel or a seal. Anchovies will eat zooplankton or larval fish. This means that when a species is removed due to overfishing, it has an effect on many other creatures, too.

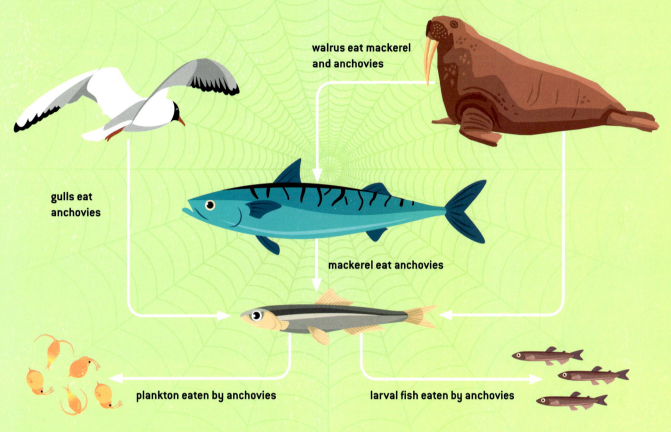

walrus eat mackerel and anchovies

gulls eat anchovies

mackerel eat anchovies

plankton eaten by anchovies

larval fish eaten by anchovies

# Recovering ecosystems

The good news is that once fish populations are left alone, they do recover. So if we stop taking too many fish out of the oceans, their numbers will increase again. We are also able to farm various types of fish without polluting rivers or the ocean.

**Numbers of cod in the North Sea are beginning to rise after being fished almost to extinction, thanks to better regulation.**

# SOLVE IT!
## SUSTAINABLE FISH FARMING

We can help avoid overfishing in the oceans by making sure we don't buy and eat types of fish whose numbers are decreasing, or that are farmed in unsustainable ways. Some freshwater fish such as tilapia are farmed in a sustainable way. Connect these five facts to design an efficient system for sustainably raising fish and growing crops at the same time.

## FACT ONE

Tilapia are freshwater fish that eat plants (including vegetable food scraps).

## FACT TWO

Plants such as lettuce need nutrients to grow.

## FACT THREE

Tilapia need clean water to live in, but like all animals they produce waste.

# FACT FOUR

By absorbing the nutrients from fish manure, plants make dirty water clean again.

# FACT FIVE

Fish poo contains the sorts of nutrients plants need.

# CAN YOU SOLVE IT?

**Think about the different elements in a sustainable system; fish food, fish waste, water and plant waste.**

Try to design a system where:

▶ The water stays clean for the fish

▶ The plants get the nutrients they need to grow

▶ No pollution is released into rivers or the ocean

Draw your design on a poster.

**Still not sure? See page 43 for a solution.**

# TEST IT!
## GROW LETTUCES IN WATER

You can grow plants without soil as long as your water contains all the necessary nutrients, and the plant has something to secure its roots to. This is called hydroponics. It can also be combined with raising fish to create a circular system called aquaponics (read more about aquaponics on page 43.)

## YOU WILL NEED

a two-litre plastic bottle

coconut coir
(available online or from garden stores)

rainwater or mineral water

a strip of cotton fabric

hydroponic plant food (suitable for use with edible plants, available online)

lettuce seeds

scissors

## STEP ①

Cut the top off the plastic bottle a couple of centimetres below where it starts to curve. The top part will be your 'plant pot', and the bottom part will hold the water.

## STEP ②

Sit the top part upside down inside the bottom part of the bottle. Thread the fabric strip through the hole in the neck, so that it runs from the bottom of the water reservoir up into the plant pot.

## STEP ③

Mix up some plant food with water according to the instructions on the bottle. Pour it into the water reservoir so the water level is below the neck of the bottle.

# STEP ④

Expand the coconut coir following the instructions on the packet, then drop a few handfuls into the plant pot. Ensure the fabric strip is running up through the middle of the coir.

# STEP ⑤

Plant three or four seeds just below the surface of the coconut coir. Put the bottle in a sunny place, keep the water level topped up and wait for your lettuces to grow! Within a couple of weeks you should see seedlings.

# STEP ⑥

If more than one seed has sprouted, remove the spare seedlings to give a single plant the space it needs to grow. When it is full size, you can harvest it and eat it!

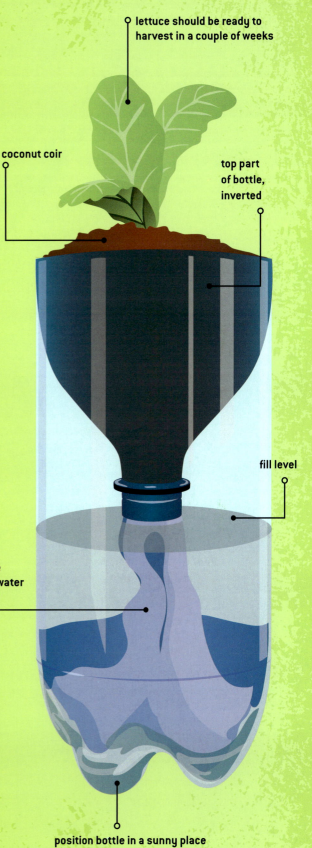

lettuce should be ready to harvest in a couple of weeks

coconut coir

top part of bottle, inverted

fill level

fabric strip dangles in the nutrient-rich water

position bottle in a sunny place

# PROBLEMS WITH PACKAGING

When we buy food from a shop, it has often come a long way to reach us. Packaging is used to protect our food and keep it fresh so that it can be sold to us in good condition; after all, no one wants to eat dirty food that has been squashed!

## Plastic mass

Unfortunately, there are a number of environmental problems caused by plastic. Globally, about a third of the plastic we use every year finds its way into our natural landscapes, including the oceans, where it creates a lot of pollution.

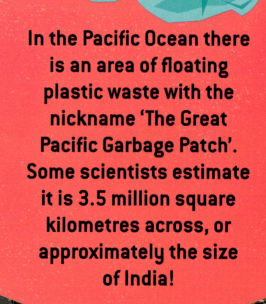

In the Pacific Ocean there is an area of floating plastic waste with the nickname 'The Great Pacific Garbage Patch'. Some scientists estimate it is 3.5 million square kilometres across, or approximately the size of India!

## Fantastic plastic

Plastic can be made into any shape or texture that is required. Because it is cheap to produce and convenient to use, plastic is often used to package food and drink that we buy on the go.

# Single-use plastic

We are using more and more plastic, especially 'single-use' plastic items such as coffee cups and plastic straws. These are used once for a very short time, and then thrown away. Though most types of plastic can be recycled, much of it isn't and ends up in landfill or the ocean.

# Lack of recycling

Globally, our low recycling rates are caused by a lack of efficient systems in place for collection and processing. It can be difficult for people to know how and where to recycle plastic items.

# ONLY 10%

of plastic items are recycled worldwide.

# DIRTY WASTE

Another problem with food packaging is that even if we improve our systems and habits, plastic can't be recycled unless it is clean. The plastic containers we use for a lot of takeaway foods for instance cannot be recycled if they have food stuck on them that is difficult to remove.

In the ocean, plastic releases toxic chemicals into the water. Marine animals accidentally eat or become tangled in plastic waste, with extremely serious effects on wildlife populations.

# PROPERTIES OF PLASTICS

What is it about plastic that means we use it for so much of our food packaging? Plastic has several different properties that make it very convenient for the task.

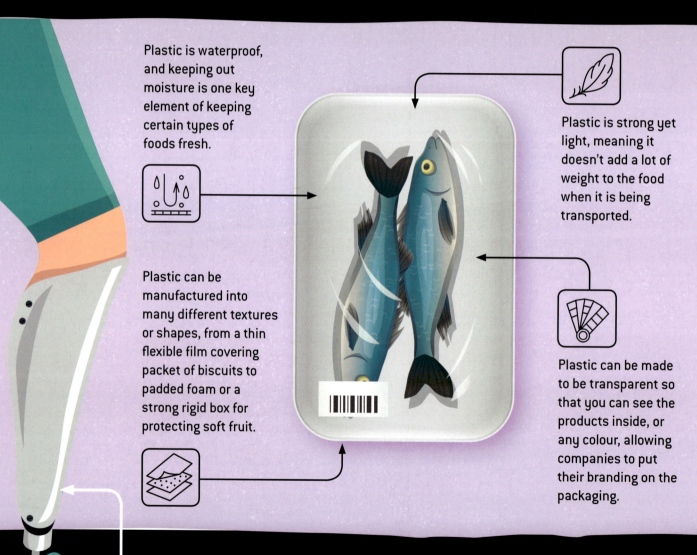

Plastic is waterproof, and keeping out moisture is one key element of keeping certain types of foods fresh.

Plastic is strong yet light, meaning it doesn't add a lot of weight to the food when it is being transported.

Plastic can be manufactured into many different textures or shapes, from a thin flexible film covering packet of biscuits to padded foam or a strong rigid box for protecting soft fruit.

Plastic can be made to be transparent so that you can see the products inside, or any colour, allowing companies to put their branding on the packaging.

## Wonder stuff

When plastic was invented at the beginning of the twentieth century, it was hailed as a wonder material – and it does allow us to make a lot of very useful items, from toys and household utensils to artificial limbs and aeroplanes.

## Around forever

One of the advantages of plastic is also its disadvantage: it doesn't break down. Plastic waste in the environment sticks around. Scientists have figured out that if plastic waste continues to be added to the ocean at the same rate as it is now, by 2050 there will be more plastic in the ocean than fish.

## Fossil fuel product

Most plastic is made from crude oil, a fossil fuel. The oil is taken from the ground where it has stored carbon for millions of years. Processing the oil into plastic involves changing its chemical structure. This releases a lot of carbon dioxide into the atmosphere which contributes to climate change.

## Compostable plastic

Scientists are developing compostable plastics made from natural materials. These plastics break down quickly, so can be used for packaging that doesn't need to last for a long time. They can be be composted along with food waste.

## Plastic from corn

Plastics made from plants such as corn instead of fossil fuels have been developed. However, while using plant-based plastic would reduce carbon emissions, recycling is still essential to avoid plastic pollution, as many plant-based plastics also do not break down easily.

# SOLVE IT!
## PREVENTING PLASTIC POLLUTION

Halting the flood of damaging plastic pollution into the ocean means changing the way we deal with plastic waste, and cutting down on the amount of plastic we use in the first place. Look at the plastic items on the opposite page. Think of some different ways we could apply the 4Rs (REDUCE, REUSE, RECYCLE, RETHINK) to solve the problem of plastic pollution.

**(1)** REDUCE the amount of plastic we use.

**(2)** REUSE plastic items again, or use them for something else.

**(3)** RECYCLE plastic into new objects.

**(4)** RETHINK the whole way we make and rely on plastic.

**plastic drinks bottle**

**plastic bag**

**plastic foam takeaway box**

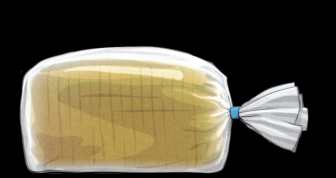

**plastic food wrap**

**plastic-lined coffee cup**

**plastic straw**

# CAN YOU SOLVE IT?

## *REDUCE  *REUSE
## *RECYCLE  *RETHINK

There are lots of ways that the items on this page could be reused, recycled, replaced with something else or made from an eco-friendly material.

▶ Design a poster showing how the 4Rs could be applied to these items so that no plastic waste ends up in landfill or in the ocean.

Stuck for ideas? Find suggestions on page 44!

# TEST IT!
## MAKE CORN PLASTIC

Renewable, plant-based plastics that scientists are developing as alternatives to those made from fossil fuels are called bioplastics. Have a go at making your own simple bioplastic at home with this experiment.

## YOU WILL NEED

sheet of aluminium foil or greaseproof paper

1 tbsp cornflour

4 tbsp water

1 tsp glycerine

1 tsp vinegar

a saucepan

a hob

a silicone spatula

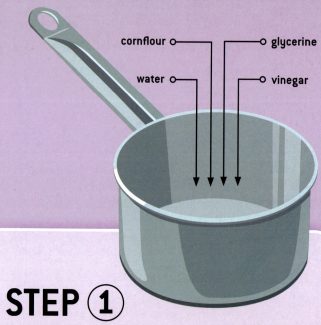

cornflour  glycerine
water  vinegar

## STEP ①

Put all the ingredients into the saucepan and mix them together thoroughly while still cold. They should create a milky-looking liquid.

## STEP ②

Place the saucepan over a low heat and stir continuously using the spatula. As the mixture heats up it should get thicker. Always ask an adult for help using the hob.

## STEP ③

When the mixture has become thick and turned translucent, turn off the heat. Allow to cool slightly.

# STEP ④

Pour the mixture out onto the foil or greaseproof paper sheet. Use the spatula to spread it out into a thin film.

# STEP ⑤

Allow the plastic to dry for at least three days. Once the plastic is fully dried, you will have a thin, flexible sheet of bioplastic.

# TAKE IT FURTHER

Why not try spreading the plastic onto a piece of gauze or fabric to make an extra-strong material? Test what happens to your plastic when you leave it in water.

## SPOTLIGHT: PLA

These cups are made from PLA, a type of bioplastic produced from corn. Its properties are similar to plastics made from crude oil (one of the most common crude-oil-based plastics is called PET). PLA can be made using standard equipment that already exists for the production of crude-oil-based plastics.

# THE ISSUE:

# FOOD WASTE

In well-off countries such as the USA, between three and four times the amount of food is produced than the population needs to feed itself. While the USA and most European countries have a huge amount of extra food, in other regions millions are struggling to get enough food to eat each day. This unequal distribution of food creates a lot of waste, and means that globally access to food is not fair. So why is food wasted in the first place?

**Roughly a third of fruit and vegetables grown are simply thrown away because they are deemed the wrong size or shape.**

## Fussy eaters

A lot of food is thrown away by supermarkets before it even reaches the shelves. Supermarkets have strict standards for how they want their fruit and veg to look, so a wonky carrot or an apple that is a bit too small won't be put on the shelves, even though the food is perfectly good to eat.

approved     approved     rejected

# IN THE KITCHEN BIN

More food gets thrown away uneaten because it goes off before we've used it. In landfill it rots producing methane gas, and because it is all mixed up with materials such as plastic, it cannot be used for anything else. Nutrients from the food that could go back into the soil are wasted.

In the UK, people throw away over seven million tonnes of food each year because they buy more than they need, or they don't know how to use it all efficiently. In the USA, 55 million tonnes is chucked each year!

**Composting turns food waste into food for plants.**

## Better solutions

Food waste can be turned into compost, instead of being sent to landfill, or it can be turned into more food – by feeding it to animals. In countries such as Japan and South Korea, pigs are fed on food waste. This was made illegal in the EU after an outbreak of foot-and-mouth disease affecting farm animals in 2001. However, if the food is cooked before being fed to the animals there is no risk of disease. Food waste could be fed to pigs, and so turned into sausages and bacon!

# DECOMPOSITION

Sending uneaten food to landfill is a big waste, and it contributes to climate change by releasing methane gas as well as not returning any nutrients to the soil. Nature doesn't create big piles of rubbish that add huge amounts of methane to the atmosphere – so what happens to plants and animals when we take people out of the equation?

## Nutrient cycling

When a plant dies, or drops its leaves, or a wild animal dies, all the nutrients and stuff it is made of are recycled through the process of decomposition. Many different types of living organism help with the decomposition process, including beetles and their larvae, woodlice, worms, fungi, moulds and bacteria. These living organisms eat or grow on dead plant or animal matter, and as they do so they help to break it down small enough to be returned to the soil.

**The constant movement of nutrients to and from living things and the soil is called the nutrient cycle.**

nutrients from rotting leaves and fruit enter the soil

plants use the nutrients to produce new growth

# Healthy soil

Soil is a mixture of minerals from rocks, water, air and organic matter from dead plants and animals which contains nutrients. The decomposition process is what puts those nutrients back in the soil where they can be used again by a new plant to grow – and then feed a new animal.

**25% AIR**

**25% WATER**

**45% MINERAL**

**5% ORGANIC**

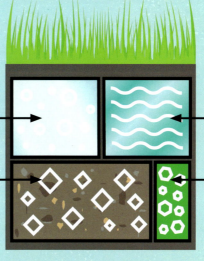

# Carbon dioxide release

Natural decomposition does release carbon dioxide into the atmosphere – however nature can deal with a certain amount of carbon dioxide in the air. This is because it is constantly recycled, by being captured and turned into plant matter as new plants grow during the process of photosynthesis.

# A problem with gas

A key difference between natural decomposition and the type of underground rotting that happens in landfill sites is that in landfill, the rotting food is not exposed to oxygen. The way that rotting foods get broken down by bacteria produces a lot of methane gas instead of carbon dioxide ($CO_2$), which is a much more damaging type of greenhouse gas, and unlike $CO_2$ is not taken up again by growing plants.

**METHANE**

**$CO_2$**

**Methane is 34 times more powerful as a greenhouse gas than carbon dioxide.**

# SOLVE IT!
## WASTE-FREE SUGAR

In natural systems there is no such thing as food waste, because everything becomes food for something else, and nutrients are cycled through the system to be used again. We can apply the same sort of thinking to our own food production processes, by composting and feeding food waste to animals. Look at all the elements involved in a small-scale, sustainable sugar production plant in South America. Can you see how to organise them into a system that doesn't produce any waste?

## FACT ONE

Sugar cane takes nutrients from the soil as it grows.

## FACT TWO

When cane is harvested, it is carried by donkeys back to the factory for processing.

## FACT THREE

The cane is prepared by first chopping the leaves off the sugary stalks.

## FACT FOUR

Donkeys have a sweet tooth, but can also digest plant fibre.

## FACT FIVE

Juice is extracted from the cane stalks, leaving behind a sweet, fibrous mush.

## FACT SIX

Juice from sugar cane is boiled. The water in the juice evaporates. Sticky foam is skimmed off the top, and eventually pure sugar is left over.

## FACT SEVEN

Donkeys produce manure, which contains nutrients good for growing plants.

# CAN YOU SOLVE IT?

**Think about each stage in this small-scale sugar production process. What is made, and what is created as 'waste' at each stage?**

▶ How can the 'waste' be made useful?

▶ Can you design a system that cycles the nutrients back around?

**Draw a diagram of the complete system with arrows showing how the nutrients are reused at each stage.**

**Still not sure? See page 45 for a solution.**

# TEST IT!
## MAKE YOUR OWN COMPOST

Compost is decomposed organic matter. Farmers and gardeners make compost and add it to the soil to help crops grow.
Make your own mini pot of usable compost with this experiment.

## YOU WILL NEED

a plastic two-litre bottle

scissors

a large handful of straw

a large handful of dry leaves, cut up into small pieces

fruit and vegetable scraps, chopped up into small pieces

a large handful of soil (taken from outside)

a piece of cloth

a large rubber band

a stick

water

## OPTIONAL:

a saucer
marigold seeds

## STEP ②

Layer up your compost. Start with a bit of soil, then a mix of straw and dry leaves, then a layer of fruit and vegetable scraps. Make a couple of layers of each type.

## STEP ①

Cut the top off the plastic bottle, so you have a tall, clear pot for making your compost in.

## STEP ③

Finish with a layer of soil on top. You want the bottle to be filled most of the way to the top, but with enough space that you can mix it up without spilling the mixture.

# STEP ④

Add some water to your bottle until the mixture is damp all the way through, but there isn't a pool of water sitting in the bottle.

# STEP ⑤

Cover the bottle with the cloth and secure it in place using the rubber band. Sit the compost bottle somewhere sunny.

# STEP ⑥

After a few days, mix up the contents of the bottle using the stick. Add more water if the mixture looks dry. Mix the contents every few days, and add water as necessary. After several weeks the mixture should turn into a dark, soil-like material.

# TAKE IT FURTHER

Once your compost is ready, trim down the sides of the bottle to around 3 cm above the compost. Poke some drainage holes in the bottom. Plant two or three marigold seeds in the compost. Place the bottle on a saucer in a sunny spot and water it. Keep the compost mixture moist and wait for the seeds to sprout.

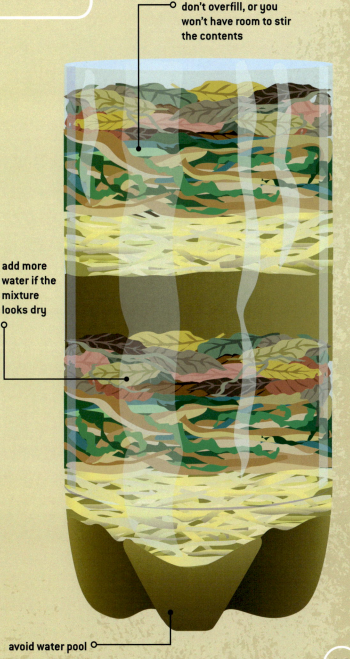

don't overfill, or you won't have room to stir the contents

add more water if the mixture looks dry

avoid water pool

# FOOD IN THE FUTURE

The ideas in this book are only some of the ways that we can change our food production techniques to live more sustainably. Scientists and engineers all over the world are working on solutions to these problems. The best solutions always take into account the most important issues locally, such as water scarcity, steep hillsides or urbanisation. Here are some other radical ways our food production could change in the future.

## Eating bugs

Would you eat a six-legged snack? Insects might become an important food source in the future. Yes, really! Although it might sound gross to eat bugs, it is already common in some countries. Food based on insects could spread around the world in the future, as they can be farmed using far less land and resources than other animals. Some products are already on the market that include protein powder made from crickets.

**Crickets contain twice as much protein as beef, as well as more essential vitamins and minerals.**

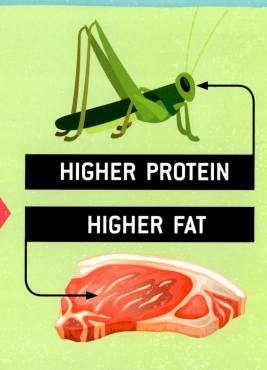

**HIGHER PROTEIN**

**HIGHER FAT**

# Insect animal feed

Whether or not humans begin to eat more insects, work is already happening to create animal and fish feed from fly larvae, which would greatly reduce the pressure on our fish stocks, and on our land and water supplies.

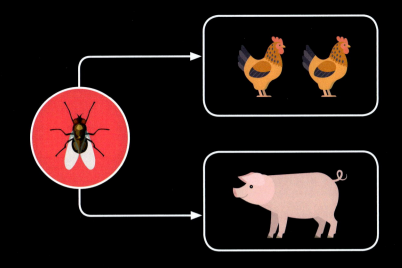

# Lab-made meat and fish

It may sound like something out of science fiction, but many companies are already developing systems to grow animal tissue – or meat – in labs. When we buy a burger from the shop it is already minced and processed, so there is no reason it needs to come from a living animal, if exactly the same combination of cells can be created in a factory. Artificial meat and fish have the potential to be less environmentally damaging, and could help meet demand for species such as tuna which are under threat.

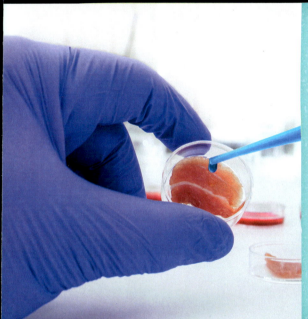

# Plant-based meat

Products with a similar texture to meat but made from plant or fungi-based proteins have been around for a number of years, but plant-based alternatives are becoming increasingly high-tech. Companies are engineering yeasts to produce different types of protein, and blending them into super-realistic meat alternatives.

# ANSWERS

**DESIGN A BALANCED MENU** PAGES 12–13

There is no one correct answer to this challenge, but here are a couple of possible menu examples that could form the basis of one day's meals.

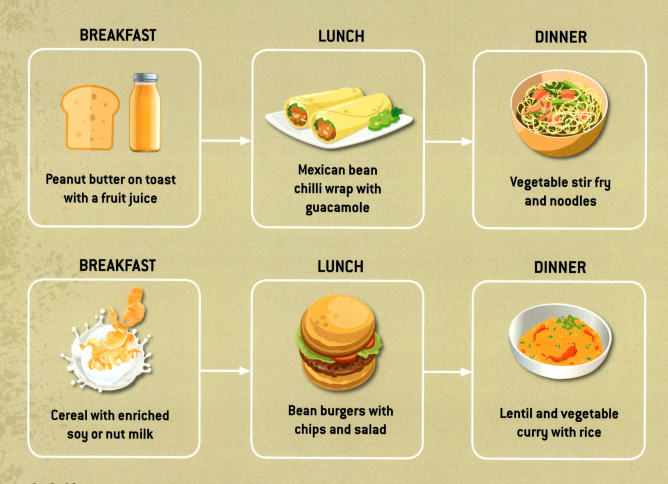

**BREAKFAST**

Peanut butter on toast with a fruit juice

**LUNCH**

Mexican bean chilli wrap with guacamole

**DINNER**

Vegetable stir fry and noodles

**BREAKFAST**

Cereal with enriched soy or nut milk

**LUNCH**

Bean burgers with chips and salad

**DINNER**

Lentil and vegetable curry with rice

## Adding supplements

When it comes to getting all the vitamins and minerals that you need, eating a wide variety of fruit and vegetables is important. There are some vitamins and minerals that are not found or are found less in plants, so people who follow entirely plant-based diets often take supplements to stay healthy. These include vitamin B12, vitamin D, selenium and iodine. If you cut out animal products entirely from your diet, it's important to make sure you are getting all of the nutrients you need.

# SOLVE IT! ➤ SUSTAINABLE FISH FARMING PAGES 20–21

A way to farm fish and grow crops at the same time in a sustainable and efficient way is by using aquaponics. This is a method of connecting a tank full of fish to a series of hydroponic (soil-free) vegetable beds.

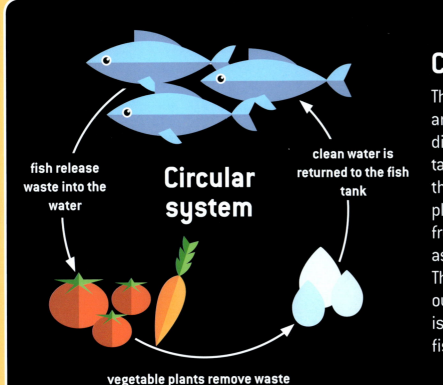

**Circular system**

fish release waste into the water

clean water is returned to the fish tank

vegetable plants remove waste by using it as fertiliser

## Circular system

The water is pumped around the system, so dirty water from the fish tank is pumped through the vegetable beds. The plants absorb the waste from the fish, which acts as fertiliser for the plants. The clean water coming out of the vegetable beds is pumped back into the fish tank.

## Fresh fish and shellfish

It's not just tilapia fish that can be raised in aquaponics systems, most freshwater fish are suitable, as well as crayfish, prawns and freshwater mussels.

# ANSWERS

All of the plastic objects on page 29 can be reused, recycled, rethought or not used at all. Here are just a few ideas for how the 4Rs could be applied to the objects.

## PLASTIC DRINKS BOTTLE

**Recycle:** Most drinks bottles are PET plastic, which is commonly recycled into new bottles, or other plastic items such as fleeces.

**Reuse:** Because air traps heat, empty plastic bottles can be used as wall and roof insulation when building new homes.

## PLASTIC FOAM TAKEAWAY BOX

**Rethink:** Takeaway containers that get covered in food are obvious candidates for new, compostable plastics. The food waste does not have to be removed from the plastic, it can simply be composted along with it.

## PLASTIC BAG

**Reduce:** Don't use plastic bags when you go to the shop. Take a reusable cotton bag with you instead.

**Reuse:** Plastic bags can be torn into strips to make plastic yarn. This can be woven into bags, hats and baskets.

## PLASTIC-LINED COFFEE CUP

**Reduce:** Many people think coffee cups are eco-friendly because they are paper on the outside. However, a thin film of plastic on the inside makes them very difficult to recycle. Why not carry your own reusable hot drinks cup instead?

## PLASTIC STRAW

**Rethink:** In the USA alone, over 500 million straws are used and thrown away every day. It's better to use paper straws instead, and better still not to use a straw at all!

# SOLVE IT! ▶ WASTE-FREE SUGAR PAGES 36–37

In this waste-free sugar production process, everything is used and nutrients are cycled back around the system.

Donkeys carry cane from the field to the factory.

Cane leaves are separated from the stalks. The stalks are pressed leaving juice and fibre.

juice

fibre

The donkeys make manure which can be used to add nurtients to the soil and fertilise the sugar cane plants.

Sweet foam, fibre and green leaves are all fed to the donkeys.

The juice is boiled, leaving sticky foam and sugar.

sticky foam

sugar

The sugar is sold as the product.

# THE BIG PICTURE

No single change to our eating habits and food production processes will solve all of the problems listed in this book. The biggest differences are made when we join all of these sustainable solutions together. So by eating fewer animal products, choosing sustainably produced food, using less packaging and recycling or composting waste, you are well on your way to saving the world through your eating habits.

## Tell people

It can seem impossible to make a difference when you are just one person. But all the successful campaigns throughout history, from social movements such as women demanding the right to vote, to environmental campaigns such as the ban on the dangerous pesticide DDT, have succeeded due to the actions of many individuals who changed their attitudes and behaviour.

## New solutions

Big environmental problems can be scary, but people are developing new and better solutions all the time. Perhaps you could come up with a new STEAM idea to help save the world?

Talk to people about environmental problems and their solutions, and you can help change other people's patterns of behaviour, too.

# GLOSSARY

**aquaponics** a system that combines growing plant crops in water without soil and raising fish

**bioplastic** a type of plastic made from biological materials such as plants, instead of fossil fuels

**carnivorous** used to describe a living thing that eats animals or insects

**climate change** a change in weather patterns and temperatures around the world, caused by human activity

**consumer** a living thing that eats other living things such as plants or animals

**crude oil** a type of thick oil found underground that was formed over millions of years from dead plants and animals

**decomposition** the process by which a substance is broken down into smaller pieces and different substances

**deforestation** the clearing, or cutting down, of woodland and forests

**ecosystem** all of the living and non-living things such as plants, animals and rocks in a particular area

**emissions** something that has been released or put out into the world, such as gases coming out of a car exhaust

**food chain** the order in which living things eat one another, starting with plants and finishing with large predators

**food web** interconnected food chains, showing how living things eat or are eaten by a wide variety of other living things

**fossil fuel** a fuel such as oil or coal that was formed over millions of years from dead plants and animals

**fresh water** water that is not salty, such as the water in rivers and lakes

**greenhouse gas** a gas in our atmosphere that traps the heat from the Sun, contributing to climate change

**hydroponics** a method for growing plants in water without soil

**landfill** large pits or piles where waste is dumped

**larval fish** newly hatched young fish

**marine** coming from or found in the sea

**monocrop** a form of farming where one type of crop is grown over a large area, year after year

**nutrients** a substance that is essential for living things to survive and grow

**obesity** having excessive body fat

**organism** an individual animal, plant or single-celled life form such as bacteria

**photosynthesis** the process by which plants make food for themselves using water, carbon dioxide and energy from the Sun

**phytoplankton** tiny plants that live in water, too small to see with the naked eye

**pollution** the presence in the environment of objects or substances that are harmful

**producer** a living thing that makes its food and nutrients through energy from the Sun

**regulation** a rule or a law enforced by a government or other large organisation

**scarcity** when there is not enough of something

**sustainable** causing no damage to the environment and so able to be maintained at the same level for a very long time

**urbanisation** the process of making an area of land more built-up

**zooplankton** tiny animals that live in water, too small to see with the naked eye

# INDEX

# TITLES IN THE SERIES